GIFTS TO SHARE

James Shields

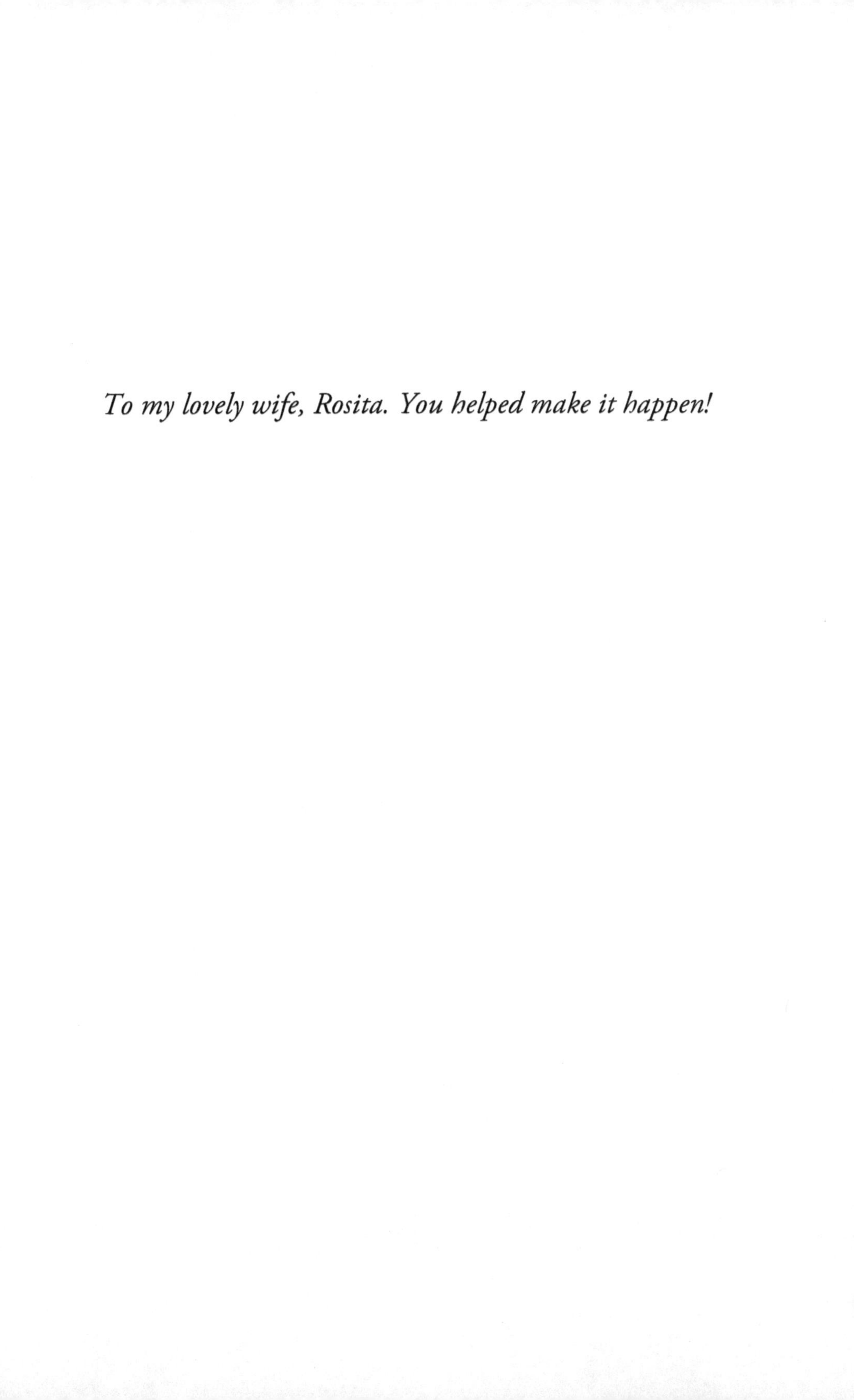

To my lovely wife, Rosita. You helped make it happen!

Acknowledgement

Many thanks to Cleda Flener for her unwavering support and assistance!

1

A full and well-blessed life is mine today.
As I walk down this garden path alone.
New daffodils reach up in rhythmic sway,
They fill the air with fragrance all their own.

Young spider shares his work in strings of glass
Upon the outstretched blades of grass are laid;
He anxiously waits there for me to pass,
Protecting crystal masterpiece he's made.

Above, woodpecker's working on his tree,
Brisk echoed cadence seems his favorite song;
His rhythm serves to somehow comfort me,
When much about my world seems sometimes wrong.

My walk was birthed in wonder from the start,
I share with you, the true love of my heart.

2

We taste white apple blossoms in the breeze
As winter chill surrenders now to spring.
God's light has touched the flowers and the trees;
The cardinal and the jay begin to sing.

Warm sunlight paints soft shadows as we pass.
We stir the somber stillness with our song,
Then place these in their homes beneath the grass,
Before life beckons us to move along.

When time has pulled the years close to her breast,
Caressing like the season's last bouquet.
And dust has marked the mortal's final rest…
What will remain of promises today?

Two lovers who will now forever be,
Together passed into eternity.

3

Summer has rainbowed ribbons in her hair,
Our meadow humming nature's favorite tunes…
Which you and I have found the time to share
And warm our hearts in sunlit days of June.

Beyond the fence life quickly passes by,
Then blurs the senses with its awkward haste;
It overlooks what we know, you and I,
Each precious moment left untouched will waste.

The sun begins to slip behind the trees,
Broad shadows reach toward us on the grass;
As one we thank our God for each of these,
The smells and sights that touch us as we pass.

One backward glimpse of wonder at the gate,
Then silently head home, the day grows late.

4

Faint footsteps shuffle slowly just outside,
As men prepare new neighbor's home next door;
Small critters scamper past our mounds to hide
Just as they've done those countless times before.

Unique the fragrance flowing on the wind,
Much like fresh furrows wafting from near field…
For some a new beginning, some an end,
When destinies and promises are sealed.

Light rain begins to moisten earthen walls
The living lower mortal shell therein,
They pause until life's yet-to-do then calls.
Time stopped and now eternity begins.

Soon evening shadows cover every stone,
And we are left together, all alone.

5

This country lane has been my faithful friend,
Meandering through the forest on its way
Past fields and farms and flowers to its bend
And where it goes from there I cannot say.

I knew well every twist and turn and trail
From kicking stones and stirring sunlit dust,
While squirrels and jays and sparrows without fail
Would play their silent games there, seems they must.

I'm told that soon the lane will meet its fate,
To feed the appetites of those who deal
In currencies of time that will not wait,
Ignoring what is value, what is real.

When all the gifts of nature have been lost…
Too late they'll realize what *progress* costs.

6

A lowly whippoorwill sings out her tune
From somewhere in the darkness, all alone,
Well hidden in the shadows of the moon
A song the forest has forever known.

Beyond, the meadow whispers with the wind
The softest message stirring in the grass;
Sunrise will mark beginning and the end
When mowers come to make their final pass.

A tuft of flowers, even in the night,
Displays a beauty eyes may never see.
Here in this place there is no wrong or right,
Enough it is to have the chance to be.

When time has taken all from man's domain,
Then nature will continue her refrain.

7

Large flakes are falling fast and free tonight,
The garden path quite quickly fills with snow,
Surrenders all its features to the white,
Hushed silence overtakes me as I go.

Behind, my footprints fill and fade away
Like shadows when the sun has passed them by,
Or smile that comes but cannot seem to stay
Or dream you can't recall though you may try.

All problems of my world are covered now
While basking in cold breathless beauty here,
Full knowing that it cannot stay somehow
For dawn will make reality more clear.

I pause and turn my face into the wind,
A warm hearth fire awaits brief journey's end.

8

The old church sets now as an empty shell,
Gray mortar on the walls is almost gone;
Front door is stuck which makes it hard to tell,
Half-opened or half-closed, the days move on.

There was a time when all was fresh and new
When air was filled with conversated sounds;
Engaging lofty thoughts, as men will do,
As mortals reach to where Divine is found.

Demise was neither planned nor plain to see…
Perhaps faith dwindled, slowly went away;
Diluted dreams of what good men could be
That disappeared like night-sounds come the day.

A lighthouse that surrendered up its glow,
Now nothing guides men past life's rocks below.

9

We climbed into the boat at His command;
He said, "You all go on, I'll meet you then."
The twelve of us, a rough and tumble band,
Began to row, not sure of where or when.

We pushed back silently, into the sun;
He disappeared quite quickly from the shore.
Not long until the waves began to run,
Our conversations silenced by the roar.

The boat soon filled with water from the sea;
In desperation we cried out His name.
Who would believe that it could ever be,
Across the stormy water, Jesus came!

In ages hence this story will be shared…
How could we ever doubt how much He cared!

10

We watch the storm put on a laser show,
The sky glows with rare pink and purple light;
Applauding thunder always lets us know
How pleased it is with nature's song tonight!

The sparrow struggles so to find its place,
As rain and wind push hard against her glide;
She darts into a bush to end the race…
Spring blossoms will provide a place to hide.

Eons of time have watched storms come and go,
With countless sparrows pressed against the rain.
And yet, it's been God's plan, for all we know,
Allow the storm, then send the sun again.

God moves according to His perfect plan,
Then leaves interpretation up to man.

11

My can-do list grows shorter every day,
This body's telling me, "Can't do, no how!"
I'm watching as my age gets in my way,
Such things I've never noticed until now.

I find myself expecting not to hear
Soft voices of the people I might see,
And even if the folks are standing near
I often smile and gesture I agree.

Not sure how much more living I should plan,
Surrounded by great things in my old age,
Just waiting for an Angel's guiding hand
To peacefully and gently turn the page.

I know that God moves at His perfect pace…
Completed in His mercy and His grace.

12

The old bridge spanned the years and river too,
Dark wood and rusty metal past their prime;
Stark evidence men did what they must do,
Providing what was needed at the time.

So often I would cross it all alone,
Heart racing as I peered down through the beams
To see the water swirling past the stones…
A farm boy making plans, and dreaming dreams.

But life could not allow it all to stay,
What men called progress brought it to an end;
Time claimed the bridge and took my youth away,
Erased like ripples floating past the bend.

Tomorrow will create what's yet to be…
The bridge and I will fade from memory.

13

How long this fence has been here, who can say,
Meandering through the meadow, past the streams,
Stones fixed and flat and pushing time away…
Like old men who sit silently and dream.

Skilled artisans set every rock in place,
Creating hedge that bordered farms and fields,
So mowers could move freely in each space…
Such are the things necessity will yield.

Creative hands have now all disappeared,
Like mist that lingers just before the dawn
That beautifies the world, but then is cleared;
It leaves its gift but is too quickly gone.

When men have moved from all that they hold dear,
My heart tells me this fence will still be here.

14

There was a patch of pine trees on our place
Far back across the creek beyond the bluff,
A most unique and truly special space
Where soft grass and cool breezes were enough.

Each season brought a fragrance all its own
I still smell yesterdays, or so it seems,
Most beautiful aroma I have known
Entwined there with each hope and every dream.

But time will turn young boys into old men…
I doubt the pine trees noticed it at all.
How I would love to see what I saw then,
To sit alone and hear the night birds call.

So blessed to be reminded of these things,
Such wonderful joy memories can bring.

15

The old mill's slicing up the fallen trees,
Selected victims of the storm last night;
As nature chose to move her hand to these
Suggests sometimes there is no wrong or right.

I heard the wind as it began to blow,
Like children's echoed voices down a well;
It turned into a sound I did not know,
Perhaps a roaring train, best I could tell.

The night began to swallow everything,
As darkness closed around me like a shroud;
Then sideways rain and hail began to sting,
I heard myself begin to pray out loud.

Deliverance was mine, through Jesus' name…
I'll never look at storms again the same.

16

I can't explain too much of nature's plan…
Earth's cycles, how the seasons change their face,
Or how the moon affects the moods of man,
Or how the hummingbird can fly in place.

How buried seeds become a plant full-grown,
How geese can know just when and where to fly,
How soil replicates whatever's sown,
How stars can cling forever to the sky.

How time can help to heal the human heart,
How God expresses love in drops of rain,
How tides know when to stop and when to start,
How gentle words can restore peace again.

God made His world, and how I marvel so…
I know that's all I really need to know.

17

The bottle bobbed upon the ocean tide,
Twisting, turning, tumbling beneath the blue…
Protecting well the message placed inside,
Like young men clinging to their brides would do.

Unknown the place or reason it was sent,
Perhaps a broken heart left on the shore,
Explaining everything their last words meant,
Then asking for one precious moment more.

Or maybe some keen traveler's silent dream,
Surrendered to a longing in their mind,
The thrill to live beyond how now may seem,
By chance a friend or lover then to find?

So many hearts love teasing destiny…
I would that such a freedom could find me.

18

I watched a sparrow as she built her nest
Of straw and grass and small pieces of string,
Arranging every part to pass the test
From every force that nature's sure to bring.

I saw her smooth and tuck down every bend,
Like mother of a newborn's gentle care;
Her patience for perfection had no end,
As she made final preparations there.

I wondered as I saw what she had done,
Could ever there a better picture be,
Of how God touches each and every one
And cares for His created majesty.

My heart was lifted as I turned to go…
A lesson straight from heaven here below.

19

For so long I had sat by the roadside,
Hoping for help as each footstep passed near.
My blindness left me with no place to hide,
Alone in darkness and consumed by fear.

I felt the warm sunlight upon my face,
And tasted swirling dust just as before.
Like many others, I had found my place,
In desperation I cried all the more.

One morning I was told Jesus was there;
He heard me call and made His way to me.
His voice then conquered every fear and care…
Praise God, His touch allowed my eyes to see!

I can't explain what Jesus did that day,
I only know He took my dark away!

20

A mass of people, far as I could see,
Each waiting there to find what He would do;
They all were hot and hungry… so were we.
No way to feed them all, everyone knew.

I spent most of the day with His small band;
I guess I was the only one prepared.
I wondered if the crowd would call His hand;
Like others there, I wondered if He cared.

His men were talking low, I could not hear.
He turned to me and asked if He could pray.
Over my meager lunch, as folks drew near,
I'll not forget those words I heard Him say!

No doubt His Father heard the prayer He said;
The multitude filled with my fish and bread.

21

I still recall the anger on that day,
A mocking, jeering crowd cried "crucify";
A soldier, I had orders to obey…
We placed on Him the cross where He would die.

My job felt different that day from the start,
Escorting one more prisoner up the hill;
His dreadful wounds and bruises touched my heart,
Deep sadness in His eyes then touched my will.

Such mayhem in Jerusalem was found;
He looked to heaven in His agony.
Through tortured, sun-cracked lips uttered this sound,
"Forgive them Father," as death set Him free.

Blood stained the cross, and dusty path He'd trod…
Quite surely this man is the Son of God!

22

Brown cornstalks stir and rattle in the wind,
No doubt a heavy frost is in the air.
Last load, then harvest picking time will end
When nothing's left but emptiness out there.

Our crop was full of wonder and surprise...
Spring rain and summer sun caressed the seeds,
Like children who've grown up before our eyes;
God's touch and nourishment is all it needs.

Reminds me of our blessings every day...
Few passing thoughts we give to time and space;
Still, nature freely gives God's best away,
Those little things that keep the human race.

Perhaps, too much I see in just one field;
Man's gratefulness should never be concealed.

23

Now, twilight and the village starts to sleep,
By following a course from eons past;
As night sounds from near forest dark and deep
Stir thoughts around blurred shadows as we pass.

Dark limbs are swaying gently overhead,
Small clouds take turns obscuring yellow moon;
It's here imagination streams are fed,
And poets find rich moments end too soon.

I'm at a loss for words to truly show
A picture of emotions I now feel…
Though lingering thoughts are quick to let me know,
Euphoria may color what is real.

The world outside may face turmoil tonight;
But now, here in this place, God makes things right.

24

Some days the doubts lay heavy on my heart,
When logic won't accept God things I know…
As questions try to tear my faith apart
And circumstances tempt me to let go.

I've often wondered, are there folks like me
Who fight life's battles hoping to receive
What He has promised: faith that's full and free,
On smother paths that help us to believe.

Eventually, through clouds I glimpse a light
That stirs my spirit like a thousand songs…
It pierces through the shadows of my night,
Confirming truths I've lived by all along.

God's Word tells us He gives each one a choice,
Discerning variations of His voice.

25

Men seek life's answers where they may be found,
Unraveling tapestries of the unknown,
Exploring every sight and every sound…
They venture into night by light they're shown.

Discoveries have happened on their way,
Along the paths that lure inquiring minds,
Mark progress at the close of every day,
Empowered by small fragments they may find.

But nature holds her secrets to her breast,
Inviting men to ponder and explore…
They celebrate and then fill in the rest
As guessing and imaginations soar.

Proceeding though reality is torn,
As superstitions wait there to be born.

26

The night is cold as snow begins to fall,
Much like the feelings deep within my soul…
Old hardness from my past has come to call,
Reminding how old grudges can control.

The darkness grows with every step I take,
I cannot see a single wisp of light…
As heaviness I've carried starts to break,
The confidence that told me I was right.

White gathers on the tree limbs overhead,
I've gone about as far as I can go…
I'll take another path for home instead,
And lay hard feelings here upon the snow.

I cannot harbor poison in my heart,
Forgiveness is the place that I must start.

27

Age leaves its mark in many disguises,
Perched high upon the currents time provides,
Bringing joy and pain and soft surprises…
Men run ahead but time always decides.

Some find fulfillment of their hopes and dreams,
When plans come together before the end,
While others feel time is too short it seems,
Missed opportunities they can't defend.

Still, fond memories like nuggets of gold
Illuminate shadowed places they find,
Offering for many a treasure to hold
Puzzle pieces floating free in their mind.

Time brushes clean every pathway of men,
As new generations wait to begin.

28

I'm hiding here in open view today,
Beyond the noise and laughter that I hear…
My heart is grieving words too bleak to say,
As sadness reaches out to pull me near.

And yet, it seems all nature does its best
To place a cheerful thought within my heart,
Inviting me to lay aside the rest,
Providing me a brand new place to start.

I sense a burst of wonder in the air!
It melts my thoughts like ice placed in the sun…
Perhaps because I've been in someone's prayer!
Maybe they'll never know the good they've done.

I can't explain what's happened here to me,
I only know my heart has been set free!

29

Then, I watched the Nation burning, burning,
And I could not believe that no one cared;
Seemed the hate was moving, churning, churning,
As I wondered, would anything be spared.

Oh! How I tried to find a friendly face,
But the fire reflected in their eyes;
Such evil had captured the human race
Set on destroying, no aim to disguise.

Remembering a time, not long ago,
When folks would work together, just to share
The gifts they had received so all would know,
Achievements birthed from differences there.

Yet freedom, when extended past its call,
Will open gates and let the nations fall!

30

Time equalizes every state of men…
It reaches out to touch each one the same,
Indifferent to what or where they've been,
Their money, status, power or their fame.

On a lark, my thoughts can wander away,
Imagining a world free of such things.
Perhaps Eden, until Man went astray…
Hard penance disobedience did bring.

Time touches beauty of all drawing breath,
Relentlessly, it claims each as its own,
And surrenders power only in death,
Then nurtures each and every seed that's sown.

A friend or foe, time is only defined
By the remnants it leaves here for mankind.

31

High I climbed upon ambition's tower,
Each rung I passed brought yet a better view…
Consumed by all the trappings of power,
I simply did the things I had to do.

On my way I forfeited all reason…
I lost the compass pointing me to right;
I followed rules that changed like the seasons,
Maneuvering between the dark and light.

I reached the top and was surprised to find
Rewards, and trappings really were quite bare…
So sad, the many joys I left behind
Far outshined everything that waited there.

I've learned that always wanting more brings pain;
*"Godliness with contentment is great gain." ***

1 Timothy 6:6 KJV

32

Hard rain came down into my life today…
I saw the dark clouds gathering at dawn;
It washed my seeds and promises away.
I prayed and prayed for it to all be gone.

I'm sure that other people needed rain,
Why should some folks be blessed and others not?
Why must my crops be harmed for someone's gain;
How then does God decide just who gets what?

Tomorrow I'll find ways to start anew…
God knows us and can call each one by name;
By faith, I'll go once more, do what I do,
Accepting that today is but one frame.

God's hands outstretched hold all the world in place…
What's best for me waits here in His embrace.

33

It seemed so long death had tormented me…
The little that I knew, I did not know;
It swarmed about my days like angry bees,
Kept whispering veiled threats that would not go.

Its cold wind churned into my thoughts each day,
Reminding me of what I had to face.
But all of my confusion went away,
When through His Word, God every fear erased!

Never again will fear control me here;
My faith rings out with Heaven's sweetest sound!
Now death is just a pause, nothing to fear,
It cannot overcome this peace I've found.

There is a place that man is blessed to find,
To leave all earthly doubts and fears behind.

34

Rows of cotton reaching out forever,
Each waiting for the chopping from my hoe;
Clearing weeds that never end, no never,
Enduring hardships man should never know.

I do my best to please the master now…
I have not felt the lash for several days;
The scars upon my back, my sweating brow,
The scars upon my soul won't heal away.

My father and his father before me,
Each toiled here for nothing but some bread;
Like them I realize I won't be free
Until they find my body cold and dead.

I heard how God delivered way back then…
I pray that He will make it so again.

35

For years we walked with Him through swirling dust,
We watched Him do the things no man could do;
Eventually we gave to Him our trust,
Amazed we were by Godly things He knew.

Then over time He stole our hearts away,
He healed the folks that others tossed aside;
We watched as the resentment grew each day,
That jealous, angry leaders could not hide.

There is no way to fully comprehend
The goodness that He brought, the love He shared…
But when He died we thought it was the end,
Abandoned there by those who should have cared.

He rose then from the tomb where He was laid,
So man could live forever, unafraid!

36

How long this river's been here, I can't say,
It could be since all time for all I know;
I guess enough to gently carve away
The edges of the world, to let it show.

If it could speak, what stories it could tell,
Of seasons and how men just come and go.
Leaving quickly, as ringing of a bell,
With what was then, continuing to grow.

I'm sure one time it flowed among the trees,
Meandering silently upon its stage…
Then slowly shaped its path when no one sees,
As everything around it turned the page.

Such comfort that I have, that men will find
This river when time's left me far behind.

37

Who can explain this story that I'll share,
Two simple rocking chairs well-worn with age,
Still on that porch, as waiting for them there…
Oblivious that time had turned the page.

I'm told they sacrificed to buy them then;
War ended as their money stream ran dry.
Two lovers who would rock and rock again,
Together, as the world just passed them by.

At dusk each day they rocked in unison;
They've never really left their chairs some say.
Most evenings the chairs still move as one,
Like part of them just never went away.

So now you've read this little tale I bring,
Reminding us we can't know everything.

38

The old mules shake their bells as if they know,
Full wagon is about to close our day;
They've learned just where to pause among the rows,
As we strip clean the stalks along the way.

We rarely speak at all, my Gramps and I,
Each deep in silent thoughts, no need to share…
To stir the silence, neither one would try,
Few words are needed for intentions there.

Long shadows say the day will soon be through.
I glance into his furrowed face to see
The sparkle in his eyes tells me it's true,
There's no place in the world he'd rather be.

There are some folks who don't seek wealth or fame,
Yet find their life's fulfillment just the same.

39

No one was ever sure where she came from;
She lived back off the road behind some trees.
Misunderstood and ostracized by some,
Such kindness she would show in spite of these.

One summer, how the sun baked all the land;
The heat dried up the ponds and then most streams.
Our well was pumping nothing but wet sand…
A time of disappointments and lost dreams.

She walked onto our dusty farm that day,
Her willow gently tucked beneath her arm.
"I really want to help" was all she'd say.
Then Grandpa said, "It can't do any harm."

And as she paced, her willow folded low…
We dug and found fresh water's all I know.

40

There is somewhere you go, where I can't be;
Each evening, as you lie upon your bed,
The places you may visit, things you see…
Surrendered to another world instead.

I watch in silence as you drift away,
Your face shares not one clue of where you go…
Perhaps a flowered meadow, who could say,
Or visiting some special scene you know.

Or maybe some sad memory retraced,
To help the healing deep within your soul,
While drifting from the realms of time and space
Quite far beyond the choices you control.

God placed in Eden, special gifts it seems,
Some remnants still come back to us as *dreams*.

41

I can't recall a time I couldn't see
White creatures placed against a sky of blue,
Imaginating all that they could be…
As lonely kids, with growing dreams, will do.

Each day would bring a new menagerie,
Soft animals that ran and jumped and played;
Engaging in such awesome reverie,
Scenes changed with time, the longer that I stayed.

But older now, I should have left behind
The joy of watching as God paints His sky,
Creating images that ease my mind,
While elephants and friends go floating by.

How much I need this lazy afternoon…
Seems grown-up voices call me all too soon.

42

That railroad track, as far as I can see,
May stretch across the world, for all I know,
Must haul the goods for all humanity…
Oh! How it rumbles, how it rattles so.

Trains lumber up the mountains over there,
Then get their speed from coming down this side.
Those stirring lights producing such a glare,
Along that path no living thing could hide.

I've never seen them stop here in our town,
I guess there is no reason that they should.
I can't recall them even slowing down;
I'm sure we'd be excited if they would.

One's coming now, like fire blazing through;
I'll chase it, not much else a dog can do.

43

We read about strange cultures and we sigh,
Consider awful things they used to do…
Small children that were set apart to die,
For reasons that seem dark to me and you.

Somewhere, somehow, somebody got it wrong.
Believing that their gods were hungry for
The lives of babies to protect the throng.
Appears appeasement always called for more.

So now we look at those and wonder how
Such cruelty could ever, ever be?
But seems the babies, folks are killing now,
Make theirs a drop of water in the sea!

Who will escape His judgement on that day…
For innocents they've killed and tossed away.

44

Somewhere on the other side of knowing,
Men searched for reasons all along the way…
Their hunger for answers always growing,
Against new questions coming every day.

Sifting through few facts that they could measure,
With tools that often caused them to misread,
Cacophonies of points they would treasure
Until new revelations claimed their seed.

And so, as time goes on and on and on…
Men peer into the dimly lit unknown,
Build on foundations of those who have gone,
Move slowly forward by the light they're shown.

Man's quest for knowledge seems to know no end,
Together we sail 'round tomorrow's bend.

45

While walking in my garden recently,
Upon the path now covered well in green…
I found a trinket lost and hard to see,
Where once another gardener had been.

Quite soon I was inclined to lay aside
All thoughts of morning planting for a while,
Just waiting for enchantment to subside…
Such possibilities then made me smile.

Did some young lover drop it as he ran
To meet the one who took his breath away?
Or maybe, it was her gift to the man,
Who filled her life with passion every day!

That simple token spoke of love gone by,
Etched there upon its surface, "*ILY*"…

46

I watched the honey bee make all her rounds,
Floating among the blossoms and the blooms;
The air was filled with perfume and the sounds
Of nectar being spread in nature's rooms.

She did not seem to give a thought to me,
Committed as she was to job at hand…
Amazed I was, that such a thing could be,
Her efforts spreading beauty in the land.

My mind was racing as I realized
The microcosmic lesson I'd been taught!
God's perfect plan for man, before my eyes:
To spread His love and joy, we surely ought!

Just like the bee, we're called to pollinate,
The harvest for His kingdom must not wait!

47

One time I tried so hard to catch the wind,
As often it would come down from the sky;
My plans and schemes to use it would not end…
I wondered why nobody else would try.

Invisible, I knew that it would be
A challenge, but what worthwhile thing is not…
I cast my net as far as I could see,
But found a breath of air was all I got.

Accepting no defeat, I would be strong,
I'd try and try and try and try again;
Eventually, decided I was wrong,
Then woke up quite fatigued from where I'd been.

Man's folly simply has no bounds it seems,
We can display it, even in our dreams.

48

Today I came upon a terrapin
Just out beyond our garden, in the grass;
I hadn't seen his like since who knows when,
Quite serendipitous that I should pass.

No doubt the little fellow was a mess,
Flipped upside down and helpless to prevail;
No other problems in his life, I'd guess
Would matter then in light of that detail.

His tiny legs fatigued from kicking air,
No longer could he hide inside his shell;
His helplessness reminded me, I'll share
Of discombobulated times as well.

I gently set him up and made his day;
Sometimes we all need help along the way.

49

It swiftly slipped across the well-kept lawn,
As evening shadows crept beyond the trees…
Pausing but for a moment, then was gone,
Was mesmerizing as late summer breeze.

I'd heard that it had visited before…
Quite often, based on stories I was told,
The remnants of a life lost in the war,
Beyond what mortal vessel then could hold.

And later, in the full moon's golden rays,
I sensed his presence near me once again;
So sad I was for all his wasted days,
Such incomplete existence his had been.

I've thought of him so many times of late…
And pray eventually he found the gate.

50

He caught a glimpse of Heaven, sure enough,
As thunderstorms lit up the evening sky…
Just sitting on his porch when things got rough.
He watched as sideways rain went flying by.

Not one to ever fear nature at all,
He settled down into his rocking chair;
Then listened as tree limbs began to fall,
Resolved that he was going to stay right there.

When suddenly, the noisy storm grew still,
The air filled with a strange and dreadful smell;
It seemed some force was challenging his will…
What happened next was more than he could tell.

Quite suddenly, ten million volts of white
Enlightened him, his choice had not been right!

51

I'll tell of when all goodness cleared away,
When men came to this country to be free;
The folks they found here really had no say…
Whites claimed the land as theirs, thought it should be.

They took advantage of the natives then,
Made promises they never planned to keep.
Destroyed, destroyed and then destroyed again,
Left many villages a smoking heap.

No doubt the Red Men tried hard to preserve
Their homes and families as well they should…
Aggressors felt they got what they deserved,
Then prayed to God just like good Christians would.

So, when they get to Heaven's golden shore,
Red Men may pray whites still aren't wanting more!

52

Our flag unfurled on Iwo Jima's hill…
The price was paid in lives and untold pain;
Honored remnants of history are still
Reminding that it could happen again.

The flag we see was raised at battle's end,
Where fearless men stepped up to give their all;
It seemed the blood and bullets had no end,
So indiscriminately they would fall.

The killing fields have since been cleaned of death,
But never would the knowing go away…
Survivors relived moments with each breath,
Confronting memories to their dying day.

We often take for granted what they've done,
Those men are surely heroes, every one!

53

Some folks find evening rain to be quite sad,
The way it tends to blot the stars and moon;
They tend to think of sunny days they've had
And feel perhaps they've ended far too soon.

But I enjoy the rhythmic sounds rain makes,
Especially beneath a roof of tin,
Or rustling sounds as spring leaves gently shake,
That stirs poetic thoughts from deep within.

Then, well beyond the simple things we see,
The moisture-laden drops help life survive,
That every living entity can be
A part of nature's clear, unending drive.

I lie in bed as sleep taps at my brain…
Enveloped in the soothing sounds of rain.

54

A building filled with bodies racked by age,
Most staring as into a memory…
Where years have left clear remnants on each page,
Awaiting news of what the rest will be.

Just walking down the hallway brings me pain
To see stark evidence of time's design;
Few here will ever walk outside again,
For dreams and years will not always align.

Stark beds now filled with bodies, broken, worn…
As *angels* dressed in uniforms do share
Then treat the tapestries of the forlorn…
Such blessings as they show love through their care!

Existing often here against their will,
Each praying the next life is kinder still.

55

What is that place where peace and love prevail,
Perhaps it lives alone in old men's dreams
Where honesty and ethics weren't for sale…
Could those days be as distant as they seem?

I've read of times when peaceful men stood fast,
When evil found no place to call its own;
Folks' faith meant trials and troubles would not last,
And locking doors and windows was unknown.

Technology has brought the world much gain
Like shutters opened wide first day of spring;
Devices that can't know of love or pain…
Such shallowness and distance they can bring.

Societies must live with choices made,
Long after debts to reason have been paid.

56

Quite amusing, or so it seems to me,
That many folks believe they've found a way
To understand all forces Heavenly,
Thus men should honor every word they say.

As if it is some awesome puzzle now,
That only the elect can understand,
But since the Holy Book teaches us how,
I simply can't believe that's what He planned.

I know quite well, through prophets long ago,
Heaven would speak to mortals here at will…
But who could doubt the Bible let's us know
Direct communications now are real.

God is aware of everything men do…
I think He wants to hear from me and you.

57

Somewhere beyond the best in class was he…
In school he breezed ahead of every grade,
Aware of all the things that he could be,
Accepting each and every accolade.

In business, it was pretty much the same;
It wasn't long until he had it all.
He found a wife to gladly take his name,
Then children came along, before his fall.

His focus was on making money first…
Did not consider all that it would cost;
One day he was confronted with the worst:
His family, his *treasures,* had been lost!

Too often such a story, folks will read,
Reminding us where *inattention* leads.

58

It wasn't that remarkable as such,
A simple act of kindness, little more,
The kind that folks don't think about too much…
Like waves that slip so silently from shore.

Dark clouds began to gather in the west,
Few noticed as the wind picked up a bit;
Soon thunder came with lightening and the rest,
Then sideways rain on top of all of it!

So cautiously she moved her rolling chair,
Seemed no one noticed from the rushing throng;
I stepped behind to help her get from there,
She smiled at me and gently sang her song.

As soon as we arrived, she disappeared…
I am convinced that Angels visit here!

59

How evening shadows love to dance and sway,
When moon begins to peek between the trees,
As limbs above keep rhythm in that way…
Soft yellow beams add form to each of these.

I've come to watch them, where they congregate
And dance this path when all of night is still…
A braver one than I might longer wait,
Ignoring tombstones weaving down the hill.

Imagination, when the sun goes down,
Confuses all you can and cannot see;
My mind keeps whispering there's things around,
Confirming what the dark keeps telling me.

Someday, somewhere, I'll think about this night…
Long after time and distance make it right.

60

His nickname back in school was "let it be",
Real pacifist as best that I could tell;
He thought his nonchalance would keep him free,
Like echoed voices floating down a well.

He would not vote, he would not choose a side,
Did not believe to do so was his place;
From every tough decision he would hide…
He walked through time without leaving a trace.

So, one day when his life was going bad,
Epiphany fell there into his head…
The things he had surrendered made him sad;
The years of fleeing life had left him dead.

True principles are anchors for the soul…
When absent, undercurrents take control.

61

There isn't much the old man hasn't seen…
Ninety-plus and he still lives every day;
I love to hear him talk of where he's been,
And of the things he's learned along the way.

He stares out whenever he remembers,
Sad thoughts of war still linger in his head;
He says, "Life is just a fading ember"…
He'd gladly do it all again, he said.

I'm awestruck by his cherished memories,
Of love and friends as years have slipped on past;
Yet though he's outlived every one of these,
He says he's found *what's perfect cannot last.*

I doubt my friend will see this winter's snow…
Fair Heaven's gain, when it's his time to go.

62

So, what then do we say to those who doubt?
The folks who won't believe that Heaven's real;
With little fear that they could be left out,
Their logic won't allow their hearts to kneel.

Intellectuals, most will claim to be
Want answers, but prefer the questions more;
Their confidence won't let their faith run free…
Hard evidence is what they're waiting for.

Truth is, what one is searching for, they'll find,
Be it doubt, or a reason to believe…
Answers grow in our heart before our mind;
Freewill then, lets us choose what we receive.

Completeness waits, the gift He freely gives.
Folks must decide the life they want to live!

63

Free speech is such an awesome blessing here…
Who then would want it any other way?
For sure, what folks have sacrificed is clear;
Our gratitude exceeds what words can say.

They fell on beaches and in jungles where
Still many lay in solemn sad repose…
Perhaps their final thoughts, a heartfelt prayer,
Undoubtedly such sacrifice yet glows.

So, why would some defile our Nation's flag,
For which those men and women gave their all…
And treat it like some dirty, useless rag!
They have the right; heroes answered that call.

Seems easy to deface and then defame,
Like spoiled children, all in Freedom's name.

64

An early springtime storm blew down last night,
Soft blanket left behind of purist snow;
Warm rays of sunshine make an awesome sight…
Where is the garden path? I think I know.

Soft crunching as I slowly move along,
Snow covered pathway stones await my touch…
When suddenly, I hear a robin's song,
Echoing past the painted tree line's hush.

Placed there beside the gate post's sheltered wood,
A tuft of flowers reaching for the sun…
So proudly there against the storm had stood,
Admiring them, I left my chores undone.

Too often I have passed this spot in haste…
Time spent with beauty rarely is a waste.

65

A single yellow flower growing there,
Beside the highway where the gravel lays…
A thousand people daily do not care,
Passing it by they go their busy ways.

The seed was hidden from the winter cold;
First rays of springtime sunlight set it free.
So graceful and so beautiful, so bold,
Growing where life is not supposed to be.

Today I paused, just to appreciate
How nature sent this special gift to man,
Reminding me that beauty need not wait,
For in its season, it will come again!

I walked away with joy and hope inside…
Given a chance, life will not be denied!

66

The night train pulled up slowly to its place;
My mom and I were pushed hard by the crowd.
The stifling car, the sadness on her face…
Cold silence stirred, as people cried out loud.

I heard the sound of bursting bombs outside;
The train would briefly stop along the way.
We prayed that we could find a place to hide…
Long hours standing, we could only pray.

Mercifully, the ride would end at dawn;
They said we would be free in just an hour.
I'll be so glad when all this war is gone…
We'll speak soon, they now want us to *shower*.

The war, the hate, the hurting and the hell…
Mankind could do no worse, best I can tell!

67

Somewhere out there, beyond the sun I'll be…
I'm sure the view will make the trip worthwhile;
Look down through clouds, to watch the rolling sea…
Those thoughts alone, enough to make me smile.

To look into uncharted galaxies,
And watch the planets course around their sun…
My mind is filled with cosmic fantasies;
When Time is past, Eternity's begun.

No more to see the hurt or feel the pain,
Or watch our world unravel at its core…
Or wonder when we'll see loved ones again,
Or question what the future has in store.

I have no doubt that I will see this place!
Forever, in the grandeur of His grace!

68

I've read about the locusts and the flies,
The frogs and all the curses sent to men!
Proved God can really do it, if He tries;
I would not want to see Him try again.

Now, modern man has their own *plagues* to bear;
They come, it seems, each time I try to sleep!
Phone-sales folks with important tales to share…
What have we done, this punishment to reap?

I haven't found a way to make them quit;
Like insects, when one goes, two more will come.
I'm losing patience, that, I will admit,
My filters have now gone from mad to numb!

The Bible says God took the plagues away…
I'm praying for His moving every day.

69

When Caesar crossed the Rubicon that day…
It was not done on impulse, not at all;
He planned his strategy along the way,
Full knowing that his fate was soon to call.

That river was not noted for its size,
A tributary at best, most agree;
Important, none-the-less he realized,
A symbol of his future it would be.

Of course, we know his army marched across,
Such firm commitment birthed his conquest then…
No going back, regardless of the cost;
The heart decides, the battle follows when.

Perhaps a pattern worth our giving thought…
Sometimes we don't move forward as we ought.

70

I'm standing here with hope someone will come,
Cardboard sign ready and I'm looking sad;
Too bad I am but charity to some,
While others look at me and just get mad.

No way I like this waiting in the heat,
But that's when they feel sorriest for me;
I then try to appear that I'm just beat,
Amazed how generous some folks can be.

The saddest part about the things I do
Is knowing that for me, it's just a game;
Quite certain there are far more than a few
Who don't get help they need, and I'm to blame.

Another day panhandling and then…
That car is slowing down, I'll try again.

71

A robin family landed on the grass,
My yard, a handy haven from the snow;
Perhaps they saw more food here as they passed,
It seemed few other places they could go.

I watched as they continued to explore,
Air filled with whiteness as they huddled near,
Then separated to find something more,
As if reminded why they gathered here.

So later, when their visit was all through,
I knew for sure there's no way they would stay;
And doing then what birds are made to do,
They found fresh fare a mile or more away.

God promised He would keep birds in His care…
We surely can find comfort, He is there!

72

We lift great telescopes into the air,
To reach far places up among the stars…
With brilliant hopes of what we'll see up there,
That helps us realize how small we are.

My mind is boggled by such awesome views…
We're seeing things man's never seen before;
Amazing and so fabulous the news,
It makes us eager to learn so much more.

Guess we'll continue searching as we can,
Accepting we can't see completely through;
I do believe it fits into God's plan,
Amusing Him, the little things we do.

Who knows what waits out there for us to find,
Created as it was, for all mankind.

73

Hard to believe, this field was once alive,
A meadow of wildflowers, so pristine…
Such special place where beauty seemed to thrive,
Where birds and butterflies were always seen.

The honey bees found nectar to their fill,
Gently delivered so, as nature planned;
Warm rays of sunlight shone each day until
Cool evening breeze came softly by God's hand.

Then men arrived, quite awestruck by the view,
Quite unlike any place they'd seen before;
They did the things that men so often do…
After a while, the meadow was no more.

What folly takes away, *wise* men replace,
Else beauty leaves our lives without a trace!

74

What is a man that God should even care?
King David asked back then, and so do I;
No doubt we find His handprint everywhere
If we will only take the time to try.

We see it in the seasons as they come,
Each bringing a fresh sense of something new,
A much welcomed beginning then for some…
Reminding us, He cares for me and you!

Invisible the course, the eagle glides,
The cardinal shields her hatchlings in the night…
Both have the need to comfort deep inside;
Like us, each one is precious in His sight.

The moon, the sun, the tides are in His hands…
A wise heart hears His voice and understands.

75

Our simple journey now comes to its end…
I hope our time together's been well spent,
Just like a pleasant visit with a friend,
When we're left wondering, where the evening went.

I've offered up my thoughts on many things,
On life and love and hope, to name a few;
I've written of the joy that sunshine brings…
How God will honor Godly things we do!

And there among the rhythms and the rhymes,
A bit of wisdom maybe did impart,
Reminding us that there is always time
To grow and share the feelings in our heart.

I do believe it's to God's glory then,
That I have shared these labors of my pen.

About the Author

Jim Shields has published numerous poetry and children's books. He lives in Lexington, KY, with his wife of 54 years. He enjoys spending time with his family, including two children and five grandchildren.

He can be reached at JimShieldsAuthor.com